The Gorgeous and Vigorous City

The Restoration of Old Eden

By

Bernard Benson Sarfo

Also by Bernard Benson Sarfo

The Fact Among Facts (1st)
The Fact Among Facts

Standalone
The Youth Murderer
Be Original Not a Copy
The Christians Science or Scholarship
Precious than Paradise
Habit Makes Future
A shelter from storm and rain
The Science of Life
The Strongest Lion Knockback
The Perfect and Inspiring City
Above Hope, Faith and Love
The Hero's Brave Decisions
The Weakest Among Plants
The Hero's Brave Decisions
Doing Above The Ability
The Wisdom Beyond Power And Greatness
Heavier Than the Heavens
The Academics Brains and Recreation Logics
The Strange Voice

The Chaotic World
Don't Miss Your Flight
Let the Nations Ponder
You Are Your Thoughts
I AM has sent me to you
Life Tools
The Fact Among Facts
You Are Glorified
The Life Cinema
The Victims of Lifelong Slavery
The Beauty behind Her Ladyship
The Gorgeous and Vigorous City

Introduction

The world was created perfectly and all the things were perfect in order. But what transpired? If you go through the bible and see what the man did, it is sad but what can we say? Why dying? Why disease?

Why hardships and many more? Why man was throw out from Eden? There are many things in the bible very difficult to understand. Why sin was permitted?

Why the tree of the knowledge of good and evil were planted? Why man was tempted only on the tree of the knowledge of good and evil but not on the tree of life?

Everything that God created has the free will. That is, man was free to make any choice. In fact, God did not force us to obey him but it is our duty to obey, because He (God) is our creator. God created the world purposely for man as his eternal home without death. And whatsoever that can cause any harm was exempted.

But God put a test before the man. Concerning the food not fit to eat, but to do away covetousness, and to see how faithful the man was. But man could not pass that test.

In fact, there are many things in the world which God purposely created to test our faithfulness to him. And to help us to develop as human beings; and to maintain our perfect character that God has put in us.

It is not God purpose to place something that can cause our ruin. But He (God) put it there to help us keep on in good works in our life.

In fact, every good thing is test by a negative to see how best that thing can last. For example, when you made a car and you want to see how best it is, you must drive it on a rough road to see the condition about that car.

If it is good or bad, that is how God did in his creation to test man who is to be an overseer of the things handled to him. The test was not like testing a machine, because the man was not made like that; therefore, the man can reason and act by his own, God gave him that chance to exercise his wish or will through an option. But what transpire?

This book will let us see our faithfulness to God and to our follow men. And also to let us, know our condition today through disobedient. Why man was sack from Eden?

There are many lessons we need to know on how sin has cost the price that nothing can pay except the blood of God (Jesus Christ). Then to know and understand the weight of every sin, committed by man.

In all, God did not leave us to perish. Yet He did something and then reestablished a new thing for future use. What will be the condition of the coming age? Who can imagine the beauty of the New Jerusalem?

No pen or human voice can explain the beauty of the mansions that Christ Jesus has prepared for His elect.

What can we compare with because it has never been in the heart of men before? This world will come to an end.

Those things that we see today will be vanished. The mansions of the day cannot be able to compare with the New Jerusalem ones.

The most magnificent city in the world today cannot be compared with. The New Jerusalem city is God made and the nature of that city will not be like today's world. That is, the present materials cannot be equal with the coming ones.

The mansions have been structured by God and the premises were His made. God created today's world with no mansion prepared for man to live in.

I mean God made it raw for man to use his ability to build for his own. But coming one will not be like that.

The structures has been built and decorated already. All the necessary things have been provided.

There will be no lack of anything useful. The structure will not be old that needs renovation or any painting to make it nice.

The state of human beings at that time will be renewing every morning. There will be no weak or old man or woman amongst this company.

Everyone who will be in this city will be fit eternally. That city (The New Jerusalem) is marvelous and the beauty of it cannot be explained.

In fact, the streets of this city have been carpeted with pure gold and the atmosphere cannot be described by today's language.

All the man made goods cannot pay for the tiniest single property of New Jerusalem. What are you searching for? What are you seeking in the today's world?

Oh my dear, will you mind and consider the coming one that supersedes everything that man can recommend?

Dedication

I dedicate this book to everyone out there and wish them all the best!

5

'When wisdom entered into your heart, and knowledge is pleasant unto your soul, discretion shall preserve you, understanding shall keep you' (Prov.2:10, 11).

Contents

1. The beginning of Grief

In the beginning, God created the heavens and the earth. The earth and everything in them purposely created for man as his eternal home.

All the things created were good and lovely. Then and again God created a garden called Eden, with all kinds of beautiful things. And the food that to sustain life was made for man.

There was nothing lacking or needful that was out which will benefit the man exempted from his life. That is, all necessary things needed were provide to make the man whole were not out.

The man and his wife were perfect in stature and exquisite. They were created in the likeness of God and the image. So, the man was like God in beauty, in stature and in perfect. God did not create this world in chaos but to dwell in peace and comfort.

Everything was in order and pleasant for the man. But God put the test that will keep his perfect being continuously before the man. Every perfect object needs to be test by a negative; to keep the uniqueness of that object and to prove the beauty of that mechanism for good performance.

You will not agree why perfect thing needs to be test; and why God created the tree of knowledge of good and the evil?

But the negative serve as the security to keep the continuous of goodness in the world. There was nothing good or perfect exempted from trials. So, every trial proofs the maturity of every perfect thing.

The world was not created without negative, but with a negative to apply our choice or the willpower. Then do not accuse God as tyrant. But to maintain fairness and order in the world, there must be a free will for everyone. That is why God does not force us to obey him, but it is our duty.

Many people want to live by sentiment and to do away law and order. I asked myself what transpire and why sorrows every day in globe? There is one thing we need to know; and to keep in mind that there can be no happiness, if we continue disregard God. Never and ever think that, God wants us to die that is why He put that tree for our test. It is not so. But He (God) needs our love and respect.

Why man was dismisse or thrown from Eden and what is the main reason? As I have already stated that man were the crown being of the universe and the overseer of the all creatures.

Those things under his control must be perfectly care and manage as to the law of God demand. But the man could not sustain his dignity as an administrator.

The reason was that he did not trust God's word as spoken to him and respected not the deity. But listening to unknown voice and done a stupid thing.

In the Garden of Eden, there was a tree of life which can keep man from dying. And in order not to experience another devil as the heaven has experienced before; God dismissed the man from Eden to prevent him from eating the tree of life; to avoid him from staying forever. So the cherubim were placed, before the tree of life with flame sword to keep the tree of life.

Here the man was throw out to go and till the ground whence he was taken. In this world, every tenant who is stubborn on his land lord would be dismissing from the house he lives.

If you could not sustain your dignity you will be a foolish at the end. Here begins mans' grief and terrible death decree. Today, many wants to live as they wish to avoid the laid down rules or obeying the word of God.

This world has the owner and we need to fear and honor him. Adam sin has brought a lot of tragedies in the world. The peak of sin is beyond control; but still many people love to commit the same sin which has damage our world.

Why misunderstanding and difficulties among us in this world? Can you imagine the dense of the sadness Adam when he was first sacked from Eden? How can you describe that hour or the condition of the man? Today's hardship can teach you a bit of the condition of the man at that moment. How do you live your life? Have you considered? Just think of it.

2. The Hardship Conditions

Why jobless; poverty, fruitless and famine? When Adam was sacked from home because of sin, there was no food outside Eden to be eaten. The man has to work for his food through sweating to get food to eat. That was his first punishment.

Outside Eden, the lands were not like the Eden vegetation; why because curse was pronounced against the rest of the land, and again there was no rain to better the growth of the planted seeds. Can you imagine the first time the man needs to search for his own food because of sin?

Consequently, the land was not rich even to yield the fruit for him immediately. So, the man needs to work hard for his own food and not like the first.

Your sin today can make a home for you tomorrow; and your stubbornness will determined the kind of hardship you must face. What do we see today and what can we do about what is going on? Can we be able to do away or ceased to sin? Why famine and poverty? Why disease and death? Why war and killings? Why misunderstanding?

Why childless and so on? Today's world wasn't like the beginning. Things have changed entirely. God created the world perfectly and orderly.

There is nothing short or to blame whether little; small or big. Then and again there was nothing without purpose whether advantage or disadvantage, they all serve for the man good. What transpire? In fact, if you look at the condition of man today testifies how sin has brought us to.

The beginning of a man was sweet and beautiful. Everything work together for only good and there was no stress in labor or sweat to the extent like today. But the man was to work for his continuous health and for good exercise to make his being fit to the standard.

The work given to man was to prolong his life and makes him sound for every day duties and the activities. The work was to give man happiness and wealth for multiplication of productions. Then and again work was to make the man improve and to develop as well.

In the Garden of Eden the man need not to till the ground or to plant for food, but to dress and to keep it. Means there was no need to work for food, but to dress and to keep the already made.

Here Adam was to preserve the fruits; herbs and the rest from the weeds, and to keep the environment from over weeds; to clean and to dress. That is to make place pleasant at all times and above all to make the Garden attractive and order.

Moreover, there wasn't any lack that needs to search for, concerning the possessions and the means. Here everything was obvious for Adam and the work given to him was cheap. There was no stress in labor or the unproductive in labor; but everything was perfect and enjoyable.

The life was beautiful; comfortable, peaceful and pleasant. In fact, Adam was fortunate than any man in the world. He was handsome and perfect in stature, fit and able man. There wasn't any comparable in creation, he was the image of God and his likeness, the first man and the manager of all the things created and above all the honorable.

It was Adam who named the creatures both living and nonliving on the earth and the air. There was harmony between the man and the creatures. There was no disturbance between the man and the nature. Everything was in order; good and beautiful.

One thing we all need to ask is who caused our problems today? Sin has been already permitted, but we can do something about it to reduce our hardship, but if we consider God and continue our submissive to Him, we shall succeed.

Today's hardship comprises our thought and acts, though Adam has caused our ruin and the death. But we are part of our problems.

There is no happiness for the sinful; but the one who keep God in mind will be keeping in peace. The peak of Adam sin has covered countless good things that can bring us joy. Every unnoticed word of God can cause us doom forever.

But the one who obey the dot; the jot or the least will be called the greatest on the earth and the heaven!

The one whose life is the best and reasonable in the sight of God is the one who consider the jot from the word of God. It is not by many words or the any word, but every word that proceeded out from God mouth will let the man live.

Adam did not consider the dot from the word of God and that caused his death penalty. Today's hardship results from yesterday disobedient, and there is no war without the source.

So the hardship condition results from unnoticed the tiniest word of God. Have you considered? Have you think about?

3. The Birth and Death

Oh! Have you ever consider the life today? What have you thought concerning birth and death? Where from this dying? In the beginning God created the heavens and the earth and the earth was formless and empty.

This world was created out from nothing, means it wasn't form from any material thing at anywhere but came as new from the creator's word.

There was a purpose of setting up this earth and the reason of that creation. Mean the world was created by God for a purpose.

The earth was created for man as his eternal home and it is exempted from any chaos, death or any other of disaster. This world was purposely designed for dwelling and beautifully planned for a man to develop it.

In Genesis Chapter 1: 28 says; and God blessed them and said to them, be fruitful and multiply and fill the earth and subdue it. This indicate that, the man and his family must develop the land and to take care of the things on it forever and ever. There was no death but birth; there was no pain in birth but peace and joy.

There was no sickness but health, and there was no disaster but peace. So, it is not God purpose for a man to die or sick in any way.

But what transpired? In fact, God gave the man mandate to give birth and to be fruitful and multiply. There was no death, or any tragedy been pronounced to the man concerning his life?

The world was perfect and beautiful ordered; peaceful atmosphere and good vegetation's everywhere. The man was capable in doing and able to control. God created the world permanently, that is eternally to be dwell forever.

In fact, this world was purposely given to a man as his eternal home with no other being. That is, not to share with any other created being. It is his house, home and property.

The man was to rule and manage as well or to have dominion over all the nature; to keep and to dress permanently. This world was his gift and home eternally. The reason was to dwell as his apartment and kingdom.

But to be a good manage or ruler, his life was subjected to two options to test his faithfulness. But the man could not pass the test; and then results the death with the birth. Now, the world has change because of sin and the live is subjected to penalties and death.

We are living with the two options; whether eternal life or death, but it depends on sowing; that determine the harvest reward. In fact, there was no death with the birth but there was an option.

There was no pain with the birth but joy. There was no severe sweat in the work, but there was fitness and wealth. There was no lost but gain, and there was no fruitless but fruitful. There was no waste but useful; and there was no unnecessary but necessary.

Everything was useful and the reason as it was to serve for good. The man and his wife were both naked but were not ashamed. There was perfect peace and joy. Oh dear, can we have this again? Sure; through submissive to the word of God.

They fit together in movement (the man and his wife) and stay in understanding and truth. There was no short or unfit in their activities and again no lack of anything needed for the life to fit as beings.

They lack nothing in their move. This world was perfect and ordered. But the man (Adam) could not maintain that atmosphere but disregard it.

In the Garden of Eden and it environment was pretty and abundant of fruits; vegetables, crops and herbs which support health and wealth. There was no need of fire to prepare or cook food.

Everything was ready when needed. There was tree of life which can keep the man eternally. The tree of knowledge of good and evil was there to keep the man faithfulness and to sustain his integrity.

There was nothing to causes the man harm if he continues to obey. They were all support his being and work together for his good; whether negative or positive; the animals, the trees and so on. There was no waste or dead thing among the nature; everything has it purpose and the functioning.

Why death instead of birth only? Why sorrow instead of joy only? Why disaster instead of peace? The world we live today has change because of disobedient and has damage because of sin.

Many people are still continuing in breaking the laws of nature as was the first man. People do not regard God but regardless through their acts and wishes.

Many people intentionally do evil and support it growth; others plan and act wrongly. The age of man has been reduced through peak of sin; and others are dying without hope.

There are alarming of death every day; people are crying day and night. Sorrow increases each day and night, and the disaster sprung up each moment.

There are sounds of fear each day and the earth cannot carry the weight of sin. Many people are going to their eternal homes because of sin and there is no hope of return.

The world is going to an end; the shadows of death have increased. The world has lost the glory and purpose of which it was created. The man was no more as from the beginning; the death has over taken the birth.

The man has lost his nature and his dominion over the earth; because of the regardless of the word of God. Have you considered?

4. The End Time Indications

In fact, this world has a lot of signs that show the dense or the peak of a sin; and the result of penalties that has cause the man. There is a sign or evidence that surely shows the end time. In fact, there is sure evidence that show the end of the world.

One thing that every man must notice or take into consideration is that, the increase of women or daughters show the end of the world. May be you will not agree with me, but it is a fact.

When woman increase, sin also increase and the world nature change to the worse state. It is evidence that, women love to promote sin than to promote good; you would not agree but it is a fact.

The women take things for granted and regardless the outcome. The world penalties today were generated through women; but in order for it to be in full or established, depends on the men endorsement. If you look at the world condition today, everything testifies that we are in the grace period. One thing that everyone must consider is the death penalty that awaiting us. We should not joke of our time but we must be considerate.

In Genesis chapter 6:1- 8 Says; when the men multiplied on the face of the ground, the daughters were born to them, the sons of God saw that the daughters of men were fair; and they took to wife such of them as they chose.

Then the Lord said, my spirit shall not abide in the man forever" When the men instigate to marry as they wish; and disregard the law of God, then comes in the increase of the daughters that promote fornication.

Many people of today think that polygamy is the way which can solve the increase of fornication and it will let some of the women not to be left out in marriage; because they are many than the men.

In fact, other people say that God does not against the marriage of many women or hate polygamy. There is nowhere in the bible that says that God support polygamy. In fact, the common sin in the world that increase each day and night than any sin that man has committed is fornication.

Many people in the world today are engaging in this sin. But polygamy is not the solution to the adultery; it's even making it worse.

The people of this world have taken things for granted and diligently disregarding the word of God. The world today has reached the harvest of distortion.

There is no truth in this world, people are hoarding up belongings and others are into serious money making. The life today is very challenging, everyone wants to become rich and live the best of life in the sight of men.

In the days of Noah, when people multiplied, the giant were born and the mighty men were in those days. The renowned men were many; and the beautiful daughters were born to them. But what cause their destruction? For the knowledge of God was reveal to them, but they disregard God and did not consider him as God. And they did not see fit to acknowledge God, but they were filled with all kinds of wickedness; covetousness, malice and full of envy. They were murders; deceptive, gossipers and boastful.

These are the acts of those days and the people committed themselves to such acts and disregard the word of God. The nature of today's act has overcome the acts of Noah's time.

Now today's world has reached the deeper state of sin. Men are hoarding up belongings and other are killing for money. Fornication has become rampant and other people murdering through lies.

There are many false prophets and false teachers today. People are making money unlawful way and so on.

These show the end time, but there is no thought in people's life today. There are many fake acts going in the churches today. Deceptions are all over everywhere in the globe. The unlawful marriages are going on; man to man, woman to woman marriages.

Many people are boastful and disrespectful, these attitude are going on everywhere in the world. These are the signs of the end time.

The women of today are moving this world into destruction; wearing indecent clothes and making eye lashes and so on.

In fact, people of today are disgraceful and covenant breakers. They love world rather than loving God. When the women increase, sin also increases. In fact, women love to promote sin rather than promoting good; they love fun and love to enjoy worldly.

In fact, the way women are making of themselves today, is horrible. And the increases of women are the indicators of the end time. The increase of knowledge is also indicator of the end time event. Wars and rumor of wars are the indicators of an endtime event.

Today's false prophets and teachers are the indicators of end time. The increase of travelers shows signs of the end. The combination of countries and the use of one currency for exchanging of goods and services is the end time signal.

The one language that is now becoming international or worldwide language shows the end time. Knowledge of a technology that is now overtaking the world shows the end time event.

The world leaders that are now finding solution for the climate change is the sign of the end. There are many things that indicate the end time, but I ask that, are you prepared to meet your God?

These signs are telling us to prepare and stand up for our salvation. The sins of this world have reached it height, and it is the time that needs to end it by God. We are in the grace period and the hour of last voice is calling. Have you considered?

5. The Wickedness of Mankind

In fact, the world has totally changed from its original state. People are confuse and do not know what to do. There are crying everywhere in the globe. Many people are suffering and dying; shouting for relief but no answer.

There are many forces and fighting everywhere; dangers are on tracks where ever you will go. Hope has gone from men and there no freedom on this earth.

There is no peace and comfort in whatever men are doing. There are wars everywhere in the globe, no sign of continuous peace. People are farther up in life and there is no complete joy.

Many people are greedy and out of satisfying in the things they want. Money has close many people's eyes and has bought their mind.

There is abundant of wickedness going on in people's life. Deceptions are flooding everywhere; and the truth has been trample on the ground. People are lying to one another and there is no favor among men. Fairness and lacks of support has lost position. There is no correct love in the world today. Many people are murdering for money and others are dying because of greediness.

There are many activities pushing men to death and some are addicted for money making. In fact, many people are out of joy because of too much of want, and others are ruining their life for ample things. Some are dying because of food and clothing.

Others are fighting on properties and so on. We do not understand each other because of money. Discrimination and stubbornness are all over the places and gossip sprung up each moment. Poor people are suffering of dishonor and do not have name in their families.

There are a lot of acts leading this world into destruction. Kindness has departed from men and corruption has taken over.

Bribe has become food all over in the world for man; we eat and store the rest. Fornication is the showbiz for the men today; and stealing has become medicine for curing our wants. Covetousness is now the king among us.

Lying is the shelter for today's world, and the murdering is the sources of income for people. Many people love money than life and honor money than God.

The world has become dark and there is no truth among us. Who will stand for the truth and who is ready for the truth?

The sins of men have fulfilled its completeness, and it is the time to end it by God. What will be your lot? Have you considered?

6. The Penalties of Sin

What is the condition of the world today? What is going on in humans' life? Is there any hope for man? Can this world survive again in the way as it was at the beginning?

Oh is there any hope for man? Why death and sorrow? Will this world be fair again? In fact, the joy of men has departed and the life of men has damage. We do not know what will happen tomorrow. Men have lost hope and courage.

The world has become dark and all the things are mourning. There is constant crying everywhere ,and the world has no peace. Many people are suffering and their joy has turn into mourning.

There is darkness everywhere in the globe. The earth cannot produce as to the best from the beginning. Our state has change and there is no absolute perfect human being on this earth.

Our days have been shortened and there is no adequate strength. Many people are dying prematurely and there is no comfort in whatever men are doing. Diseases have spread all over the world and there is no balm for perfect healing.

Men are into much troubles and happiness has vanished. Many people cannot sleep soundly because want; and others are into much trouble because of their destitute state.

We cannot enjoy the life to its best. Fear has taken people's mind and there is no perfect peace. There is no perfect hope but always fear of want and discouragement.

Things have fallen apart and others are mourning bitterly. Sorrows upon sorrow are growing here and there. There are wars and rumor of wars. Sudden death and disasters are happening here and there.

Hurricanes and the earthquakes are happening rampant here and there. There many things difficult to understand are happening each day and night. Can all these things ceased? Sure! There is a solution and hope for men again.

Many people are desperate and have lost hope concerning this age. But there is a joy after labor and there is a peace after the victory of war. What we are seeing and hearing is the cause of sin. But God will bring these things into an end and this world will take it fine cloth again.

Let's consider this scripture; Matthew 24:29-31, 32-35 (King James Version)

Immediately after the tribulation of those days shall the sun be darkened, and the moon shall not give her light, and the stars shall fall from heaven, and the powers of the heavens shall be

shaken: *and then shall appear the sign of the Son of man in heaven: and then shall* all the tribes of the earth mourn, and they shall see the Son of man coming in the clouds of heaven with power and great glory.

And he shall send his angels with a great sound of a trumpet, and they shall gather together his elect from the four winds, from one end of heaven to the other.

Now learn a parable of the fig tree; when his branch is about to tender, and putteth forth leaves, ye know that summer *is* nigh: so likewise ye, when ye shall see all these things, know that it is near, *even* at the doors.

Verily I say unto you, this generation shall not pass, till all these things are fulfilled. Heaven and earth shall pass away, but my words shall not pass away.

The sin has caused us a lot and has damage everything in the world. Men what are we doing? Shall we continue in sin or continue in wrong doing? Sin shall kill the sinners and God will destroy those who destroy the earth. You have considered?

7. The Inside Eden

The world was created perfectly and beautiful by God. Everything works together for the man good. Peace reigned and the world was calm and pleasant. It was created for the man (Adam) and his wife.

It is well and good with no decay or stain whatever in the world whether negative or positive. It was Adam who named all the animals and the other things. God prepared the best home for Adam and his wife called the Garden of Eden.

There was harmony in everything and the world was great in beauty. There wasn't any want or needy. There were trees fit to eat its fruit and beautiful at sight.

There were tree of life and tree of knowledge of good and of evil. These things were created to serve the man good and to help him to prosper. There was no hard labor but to dress and to keep the garden.

This is to let man fit and to be continuous healthy. There were rivers fit for consumption and beautiful. The place was superb and comfortable with no likens. Have you imagined such a condition and the state?

In fact, there wasn't any home like that, very gorgeous and healthy. There were a lot of others things that serve as an entertainment materials for the man good. The man was the crown being of all the created things.

There wasn't any lacking but abundant and beautiful. There was no need of farming for the production of food or till the land for food production. In fact, there were abundant fruits and herbs that can serve man eternity without want. Let's consider this scripture;

And God said, Behold, I have given you every herb bearing seed, which *is* upon the face of all the earth, and every tree, in the which *is* the fruit of a tree yielding seed ; to you it shall be for meat. And to every beast of the earth, and to every fowl of the air, and to everything that creepeth upon the earth, wherein *there is* life, *I have given* every green herb for meat: and it was so. And God saw everything that he had made, and, behold, *it was* very good. And the evening and the morning were the sixth day.

Genesis 2:29-31(King James Version)

The man and his wife were at peace, there were no misunderstandings between them. They were naked but not ashamed of themselves. There was a perfect love and understanding. There wasn't anything called a disease or sickness.

The man and his were fit and sound in appearance. The human history was with only good and perfectness, but what happened? Man and his wife disobey God and everything change.

Now what do we see and hear? Have you considered? Oh men, we need to be careful and behave as the law of God requires. We need not to continue in what our first parent did and thrown out from their beautiful home. Let's consider our doings and stay as the law of God requires.

8. Yes or No Principle

The world has the beginning and the basic foundation of every creation. In the beginning, God created the heavens and the earth, and the earth was formless and void. This earth was formless and void but God refine it by his word.

The things of this world have its start and the basic foundations. In fact, the truth is that, there was nothing which has change as from the beginning from their original state.

The laws controlled this world or there are rules and regulations governed this world. The world cannot function without these laws. God created this world with the laws.

The world was perfect and beautiful. There was no decay or stain on those things created. And God saw that everything he has made was superb.

There are basic foundations of all the things created. In fact, God word is productive and eternal. Everything that God created have its kind; purpose, benefit and functions. There were positive and negative things.

All these things were created to serve the man good. In fact, the negative ones are not bad ones, but to serve the purpose and to make the others efficient.

It is God purpose to make this world the eternal property for man. But the purpose was dissolved by man. The man was given the free will to decide for his own and to choose his wish.

But God put good and evil before him to test his loyalty and respect, own for his word. But the man rejected the word of God and went for his own wish.

The world and everything in them was for the man good. The basic principle of this world is remaining till now; nothing has changed. We need to understand that, the natures of this world remain the same. Nothing has changed from its natural state.

Some people want to change what God has established from the beginning and to misplace what is in place. What God has said, can't be change by man? Do not add or remove and find you are an untruth. What did the word of says?

In the beginning, God created the heavens and the earth. Were the heaven, and the earth was created by God? Yes. Does this world have been disappearing? No. Does God created the things in this world in six literal days? Yes! Does God created the sea and everything in them?

Yes! Has the sea has been disappearing? No! Does God bless the seventh day? Yes! Were the tree of life and the tree of knowledge and of good and evil created by God in the Garden of Eden? Yes!

Who did God created in his own image and likeness? (Adam). Do God created animals and birds? Yes! Are they productive? Yes! And God said to them, be fruitful and multiply. Can birds produce tress? No! Does the creation have stop production? No!

The basic thing in the kingdom of God is to obey, the word yes or no. there is no question to ask or there is no need of explanation or interpretation. Just obey the word yes or no.

Many people of wants to worship God in the way they wish or suit their favor. Others want to do away the truth as established from the beginning. They want to change the foundation already built. You cannot do away what God has established from the beginning of creation.

In fact, the death penalty today, was from disobedient of Adam. What did God said concerning the tree of knowledge of good and of evil?

Do not touch it or do not eat of it. That is all, there shouldn't be any question. Just obey what you have been told. Today Christians want to establish their own thing; for their favor.

They want to do away the foundation already built by God and to do their own thing or establish their own. What do I mean? The day of worship has been established by God but they have established the new one for God to obey them, than to obey God.

They have exchange the God who created the heavens and the earth and have replaced themselves as God. Every institution that is contrary to what God has established is against God government. Example marriage is for man and woman. Not man for man or woman for woman. So it is, on the day of worship.

You cannot place the first day for the seventh day as the day for worship God who created the heavens and the earth. Does God told us to remember the first day?

No! Does God told us to remember the seventh day? Yes! Why do some Christians honor the first day as the day of worship or rest, instead the seventh day?

In fact, the basic truth is that; there is nothing in creation that has change from its original state. But human beings want to do away the mothers of creation.

What did the word of God says? Do not touch it or eat from the tree, but the Adam and his wife did not obey. Now we are dying because of disobedient. Shall we continue in disobeying as did Adam and his wife?

What is my main concern on this content: (Yes or No Principle) Christianity is not about comments or explanation of our views or doing what you think is good in your own sight? You cannot teach God or show him the right way of doing things. Who are you to teach God what is right?

Today so called Christians want to establish their own law and to abolish what God has established. The earth is the mother of all things. Means all things come from the earth. If the earth is remove, all things will be affected or vanish. God created this world and everything in them for a purpose. And it is also governed by laws.

If you do these laws away, you cause confusion to the things that were created. It was Adam who named the things of this world. And the names that were given by Adam were still remaining the same.

So, who are you to change these names? Or do away the original ones. Many Christians of today want to do their own thing, by establishing counterfeit to substitute the original. In fact, as you cannot replace man as woman, so you cannot replace false as true.

In fact, the one who want to walk wards is practicing abomination. So as to the one who want to change his or her nature humanity. In fact, falsehood is ruling the world today.

And the Christians who must tell the truth have joined the hands with the devil and fighting against the truth. There is no truth in this world. People love to do their own thing, instead of what God has commanded them.

We need to obey the word of God whether it is left or right; we must obey the word yes or no. there shouldn't be any question or comments on that. What do the word of God says?

You shall not eat of it; neither shall you touch it, lest you die. Here the word of God says; they should not eat from the tree of knowledge and of good and evil. Many people want to do away the mothers of creation. That is, they want to question what God has create and said.

This is stubbornness and unbelief. There shouldn't be any question or comments concerning the word of God. Why because we don't have any idea or knowledge concerning the creations of God. As human beings, we need to be very careful on how we respond to the word of God. What do I want us to share or study?

The basic true religion has been already establish by God; and there no way to add or change it. From Adam to Noah, Abraham and to the last born of human being, God word is remaining the same.

Whatever has proceeded out from God's mouth is eternal. God does not change his word and of its kind. Every word of God will let man live.

Any word of God that was said to Israel, he is saying the same word to us again.

O man, what *is* good; and what does the Lord require of you, but to do justly, and to love mercy, and to walk humbly with thy God? (Micah 6:8)

The true foundation has been already built and all the blocks that fit for laying has been already made. There is no need of any block again to build the full house of the faith.

Were the things of the world remaining the same? Yes. You cannot use gold as silver; neither can you use silver as gold. You cannot use first day as a seventh- day; neither can you use seventh-day as a first day.

You cannot compare God with any object; neither can you compare any object with God. Do not be deceived by the devil or anyone. What God has said, is remaining the same.

Let your yes be yes and your no be no. anything more than this is evil. The word of God is remaining the same. Let's maintain it as it is, so that, we will not be find as an unfaithful steward. Have you considered?

9. The New Heaven and New Earth

The history of a man on this world today will be forever end. The sin of Adam and its penalty will be ended. The sky and earth that we see will be change and replace by new one.

Today's world has been polluted by sin and all activities of men. In the beginning God created the Heavens and the Earth and God prepare the Earth for man as his home.

This world was purposely created for man as his property eternally. It was without sin and death; comfortable atmosphere reigns. It was gorgeous and fabulous to behold.

Now many things testify. But sin has damage everything from it beauty and perfect. It is not God's will that our world will damage by sin. But man disobey God instruction and make it void.

So, it has become necessary for God to make new one for those who obey and love Him. The sin that has been damage this Earth must be root out for eternity.

The whole nature has been damage and polluted by sin. The Angel who brought this sin from Heaven must be punish and destroy for eternity. He is here on Earth causing our ruin day and night. His time is now up for him to be removing from this Earth forever.

This battle will be great and fearful for man who has committed sin with the devil. It is his punishment but not a man but God will destroy those who destroy the Earth with this devil.

It is God's wish that this Earth that has been polluted by sin will be removed and then restore new one. The Bible make it clear that the new Earth and Heaven will be establish and the old one shall not be remember again.

So, this world will be restoring by new one. Let's read Revelation 21:1, 2

Read;

Now I saw a new heaven and a new earth, for the first heaven and the first earth had passed away. Also there was no more sea.

2Then I, John, saw the holy city, New Jerusalem, coming down out of heaven from God, prepared as a bride adorned for her husband.

The world today as we see will remove and then restore by a new one. John; the revelator saw the new heaven and the new earth and old one had passed away; and the sea which we see today will be no more. In fact, God will bring the new heaven and the new earth that supersedes the old one. That is today's one, and it shall be not remember again.

As God at the beginning created the heaven and the earth for man and his descendants, so He shall create new one for those who obey and love Him.

This new heaven and new earth will be different from today's one. There will be no more sea but different one. This new world will not contain raw materials that need refinement but useful one ready to use.

God will establish His kingdom within this new world for eternity. There will no more sickness; no more pain, no more poverty, no more envy, death and others.

All things will be made new and fit for endless age. What the Bible has said is true and there is no doubt about it. Death shall no more exist and our lives will be fruitful for eternity.

In fact, the world today cannot be compare to the coming one. Today's vanity life will not be part; our life will be comfort and necessary.

God will not create new human beings as His likeness and image like the old. But God will restore His nature that we lost at the beginning because of disobedient. We shall be like Him and shall be like us eternally. Consider this text and read.

Revelation 21:3, and 4.

Read;

3And I heard a loud voice from heaven saying, "Behold, the tabernacle of God is with men, and He will dwell with them, and they shall be His people. God Himself will be with them and be their God.

4And God will wipe away every tear from their eyes; there shall be no more death, nor sorrow, nor crying. There shall be no more pain, for the former things have passed away."

This new world will be different from today's world. God tabernacle will be with us and He shall dwell with and shall wipe away our tears from our eyes. This means we shall be comforted with the presence of God and enjoy with Him throughout eternity.

He will not leave us; our eyes shall see Him with the endless age. Do you wish to be part with the saints on this new heaven and the new earth?

10. The state of the Saints

God form the man from the ground and made him resemble to His image and likeness at the beginning of creation. A man was made in the likeness of God; perfect and handsome.

He (Man) holds the beauty and the glory of God. All things that were created were his charge, to care and have dominion of them. He has the ability to control and manage.

He was out of hate and death. Well balance in his doings. What can we imagine concerning the nature of a man at the beginning of creation? Adam resembles God in likeness and image.

There was no short of him that degrades his ability to do as God's son or image. He holds the character of God and glory. In fact, man was perfect and handsome as well.

He was a crown being the earth and the ruler of the things that were created. He lost his state as a crown being through disobedient.

He was sacked from his home and became as nothing. His state that resembles God changed and polluted by sin committed. Now the image and likeness of God became short and degraded. Adam became the image of the devil and the likeness of his (devil) doings.

Our hope as human beings lost and man became alone of no mediator. The image of God is now the image of the devil. Jesus look at our condition and it troubles His heart.

Who shall redeem the man from this condition? The condition of man was abysmal and challenging. Now the state of a man has been subjected to sin and death.

Christ Jesus decided to die and restore the image of God that man has lost. He (Christ Jesus) became a man and lived among men for the man sake.

God is eternal God and whatever He creates must be an eternal thing. So, the man was to live as God eternally. This condition was lost by the sin of Adam (The first Man).

The death of Christ has restored the glory and the image of God that man loss through sin. Now this restoration comes by accepting Jesus as your personal savior.

In fact, the old image and likeness of God that man lost; will be regain and restore for eternity by the coming of Christ in the second time.

This condition will last eternally. The state of the saints will be the first image and likeness of God that man lost. The saints' lives will be God's lives and shall be as God forever and ever.

They will be fit as God throughout eternally. Their lives will be free from pain; weakness, worrisome, diseases and death.

There shall be no poor man or woman among them. No servant or maid in this company. Their life will be joy forever.

There shall be no more house rent; no more light and water bills, no more school fees, no more transport fairs, no more widow, no more child disturbances and others.

Their condition will be comfort and free from anything that cause cry or sorrow for everlasting. In fact, the saints shall sit as God who does not die nor slumber. Do you wish to become one or be among this group?

Let's read some condition they will be in the New Jerusalem.

Isaiah 65:17 -24

Read;

17"For behold, I create new heavens and a new earth; and the former shall not be remembered or come to mind.

18But be glad and rejoice forever in what I create; for behold, I create Jerusalem as a rejoicing, and her people a joy.

19I will rejoice in Jerusalem, and joy in my people; the voice of weeping shall no longer be heard in her, nor the voice of crying.

20"No more shall an infant from there live but a few days, Nor an old man who has not fulfilled his days; For the child shall die one hundred years old, But the sinner being one hundred years old shall be accursed.

21They shall build houses and inhabit them; they shall plant vineyards and eat their fruit.

22They shall not build and another inhabit; they shall not plant and another eat; for as the days of a tree, so shall be the days of my people, And My elect shall long enjoy the work of their hands.

23They shall not labor in vain, nor bring forth children for trouble; for they shall be the descendants of the blessed of the LORD, and their offspring with them.

24"It shall come to pass that before they call, I will answer; and while they are still speaking, I will hear.

The saints will no longer suffer for wants but their life will be eternal joy. What the Isaiah is saying testifies the absences of death and other sufferings. So, the saints of God will have His image and likeness that Adam (the first man) lost. They shall enjoy life for time without end.

The state of the saints will be happiness and shall resemble God's in character; in beauty, in fitness, in the image and glory. The old nature will no longer inherit and previous things will no longer be remembered.

My dear reader, what is your decision today? Will you accept Christ Jesus as your personal redeemer? Do you wish to be among this group? God wants to restore His image that Adam lost for the second time and then enjoy life with ceaseless age. Will you mind?

11. The State of New Jerusalem

God has chosen Jerusalem as the name of the coming city. This shows the love of God towards mankind. Jerusalem on earth today as the city of Israel will be the name of New Jerusalem that God prepared for His people.

Why God chose that name and what is stand for? David became king on Israel some time ago. His kingdom must last for ages to come.

This kingdom must be continuing by his seed that devoted his life for the world. It is God intention that man shall live eternally for the first time He created him.

We lost this opportunity because of sin. Jesus accepted to restore what was lost for man. Here, the world created for man sake as his property forever. Through disobedient of Adam, the idea of God lost and became hopeless.

Who will restore such a condition that has been occurred? God chose Abraham and his seed to let the world know who He is. He gave birth to Isaac and Isaac also born Jacob and Jacob had twelve sons. The eleventh son was sold and sent to Egypt. Judah the fourth son devoted his life for his younger brother in Egypt when they were tested by their brother Joseph. His act was amazed; so the savior of the world was born to this family.

David the king came from this family and his seed must continue his kingdom that has been promised by God to be an everlasting kingdom. Intentionally, God created the world for man and it must rule by a man.

Jesus became a man and lived among men. He was the son of David and kingdom of David must be there for eternity. David ruled his kingdom in Jerusalem as his capital city.

It is interesting to note that God choose this same name for His son Kingdom. This means that, God is faithful in all his promises and sayings. Jerusalem must last eternally than all cities in the world today.

This is the love of God towards mankind. Now the state of the New Jerusalem: What will be the condition of this state?

Let's consider this text from Isaiah 65:17-19

Read;

17"For behold, I create new heavens and a new earth; and the former shall not be remembered or come to mind.

18But be glad and rejoice forever in what I create; for behold, I create Jerusalem as a rejoicing, and her people a joy.

19I will rejoice in Jerusalem, and joy in my people; the voice of weeping shall no longer be heard in her, nor the voice of crying.

Jerusalem will be a rejoicing city and her people a joy. It has been prepared like a bride for her husband. The city holds the glory of God and He shall dwell in it with His people. It is a great and holy city.

Now consider the nature and the beauty of this city phase by phase. In fact, the beauty of this city has no equal. It has never come to mind or heart that which God has prepared for His love ones. Let us read from the Bible Revelation 21:10 onwards to 22:1-7: read;

10And he carried me away in the Spirit to a great and high mountain, and showed me the great city, the holy Jerusalem, descending out of heaven from God,

John was carried in the Spirit to a great and high mountain and he was shown the great city, the holy Jerusalem descending from God out of heaven.

The city of God's people has been already built from heaven and it has been prepared like a bride for her husband.

In fact, Jerusalem will appear in heaven and then descending to the earth with glory and honor. See how wonderful God is! He can build in the air and descend it on the ground for the sake of His people.

What is your problem? What are you searching for? Will you consider this? Read verse 11, 12 and 13 and then take note of the city state.

11having the glory of God. Her light was like a most precious stone, like a jasper stone, clear as crystal.

12Also she had a great and high wall with twelve gates, and twelve angels at the gates, and names written on them, which are the names of the twelve tribes of the children of Israel:

13three gates on the east, three gates on the north, three gates on the south, and three gates on the west.

It has the glory of God and her light was like a precious stone, clear as crystal. The great and high wall has been built around it and three gates with all the four corners and the twelve angels at the gates.

This means that, there will order and peace of all up coming and going. What can you compare with this scene that the revelator (John) saw in his vision?

This is wonder and interesting scene. Today's glorious city in the world is rag before this city the New Jerusalem. Read verse 14; 15 and 16 and then think of description of this city.

14Now the wall of the city had twelve foundations, and on them were the names of the twelve apostles of the Lamb.

15And he who talked with me had a gold reed to measure the city, its gates, and its wall.

16The city is laid out as a square; its length is as great as its breadth. And he measured the city with the reed: twelve thousand furlongs. Its length, breadth, and height are equal.

John saw the foundation under the main wall and it has twelve different kinds and the names of the apostles written on them.

This is great recognition and the love of Christ to His friends (the Apostles). The city was measured by the angel and all the sizes are equal in length; breadth and the height.

It is a square city with the length of each side twelve thousand furlongs. Have you considered? Continue the reading verse 17; 18 and 19 for more insight.

17Then he measured its wall: one hundred and forty-four cubits, according to the measure of a man, that is, of an angel.

18The construction of its wall was of jasper; and the city was pure gold, like clear glass.

19The foundations of the wall of the city were adorned with all kinds of precious stones: the first foundation was jasper, the second sapphire, the third chalcedony, the fourth emerald,

Did you observe the kinds of the foundations about this city? How have you take note? It is adorned with different kinds of stones; like jasper, sapphire, chalcedony and the emerald.

It is decorated with pure gold, like clear glass as well. Oh! What a marvelous city! How wonderful love that Christ has shown to us as His people?

He died on the cross and suffered for us to receive this city that was prepared from the foundation of this earth.

God is taking His dwelling city to this earth for the sake of man. Oh my dear, can you imagine such a wonderful love that God has reveal towards us. What again? Read verse 20; 21, 22 and 23 and think of it beauty and perfect.

20the fifth sardonyx, the sixth sardius, the seventh chrysolite, the eighth beryl, the ninth topaz, the tenth chrysoprase, the eleventh jacinth, and the twelfth amethyst.

21The twelve gates were twelve pearls: each individual gate was of one pearl. And the street of the city was pure gold, like transparent glass.

22But I saw no temple in it, for the Lord God Almighty and the Lamb are its temple.

23The city had no need of the sun or of the moon to shine in it, for the glory of God illuminated it. The Lamb is its light.

God and Lamb will be our temple; so there will be no temple in it. The streets will be gold streets pure and transparent glass.

There shall be no light but God glory will be our light and of the Lamb. Sun and moon will be absent. The twelve gates were twelve pearls: each individual gate was of one pearl.

You deserve it because Christ has paid for you to dwell in this city. Read 24 to 27 and decide your future now.

24And the nations of those who are saved shall walk in its light, and the kings of the earth bring their glory and honor into it.

25Its gates shall not be shut at all by day (there shall be no night there).

26And they shall bring the glory and the honor of the nations into it.

27But there shall by no means enter it anything that defiles, or causes an abomination or a lie, but only those who are written in the Lamb's Book of Life.

Those who are saved shall walk in its light and the kings of the earth shall bring their honor and glory in it. The gates will not be shut all the day and it will one day; because night will not be present but days; years will be seen and know.

This is not just a dream but real and it is coming for those who deserve it and have prepared for it. Do you believe? What are you doing towards it? Is this your aim and desire?

What again do you wish to know about this city? What is revealed is for us and our children. But those hiding ones are for God. How have you take this message? Read chapter 22 and see some unique things about this city again. Read verse 1 to 3 and then continue on the discussion.

22And he showed me a pure river of water of life, clear as crystal, proceeding from the throne of God and of the Lamb.

2In the middle of its street, and on either side of the river, was the tree of life, which bore twelve fruits, each tree yielding its fruit every month. The leaves of the tree were for the healing of the nations.

3And there shall be no more curse, but the throne of God and of the Lamb shall be in it, and His servants shall serve Him.

There was a water of life in this city clear as crystal, proceeding from the throne of and of the Lamb. It is in the middle of the streets, there was the tree of life which Adam was bound not to eat from it when he first sin.

This tree bore twelve different kinds of fruits and heals the nations by it leaves. It also yields fruit every month. What can you compare and think off?

It has never been in the heart of men or thought off those things that God has prepared for His children. Read verse 4 to 7 and prepare yourself for this coming new world.

4They shall see His face, and His name shall be on their foreheads.

5There shall be no night there: They need no lamp nor light of the sun, for the Lord God gives them light. And they shall reign forever and ever.

6Then he said to me, "These words are faithful and true." And the Lord God of the holy prophets sent His angel to show His servants the things which must shortly take place.

7"Behold, I am coming quickly! Blessed is he who keeps the words of the prophecy of this book."

The state of New Jerusalem is wonderful and there is nothing that can be compared with. Our ways are not God ways, neither our thoughts are His thought.

As the heaven is higher than earth, so God's thought are higher than us. For He knows thoughts He thinks towards us, not the thoughts of evil but the thought of peace and future expectation.

This city the New Jerusalem has been already built. It has the glory of God and of the Lamb. There shall be no night there and the light will not be necessary in it.

Gold shall be our carpet on our foot. Cars will be useless and airplane will not be needed. There are a lot to comment with but time will not permit me to say more again. I know you have read a lot and it is sufficient for your life.

12. The Everlasting City

Why everlasting city? Will it collapse? Will there be any city again? What this city stands for? Who will be the leader; the king or the president of this city?

What job shall the saints will do? What will you do if this city becomes yours? If you ask me, I cannot answer you now. But today's life will determine tomorrow's destiny.

It is a challenge to you and must seriously decide your stand today for the coming city (the New Jerusalem).

Who must enter this city or have chance to be in this city? If you believe it or not, it is going to come. God is eternal God and whatever He creates is an eternal thing.

But sin destroys the nature of everything that is eternal. Means there is nothing that can destroy any created being but sin. So, God will destroy sin and sinner for eternity.

New Jerusalem will not be entered with anything that is sin. Those murderers; sexually immoral, idolaters, and whoever loves and practices a lie will be outside of the city. Sin will not be part in this city.

There will be no anything that will be the test for saints. The city will contain only good; perfect and precious things. Christ Jesus will be the leader; the king and president in this city. The city holds the glory of the Lord and of the Lamb. It is dwells justice and righteousness.

Those who dwell in have the character; the image and the likeness of God. There will be no second devil; for the former things are over and shall not be remembered.

There will be no lack; poverty, disease or anything such like that. For things are make new and former ones are forever forgetting. This city has no end and it will be there for countless age.

It is the city of God and it cannot be destroy or collapse. For God is eternal God and everlasting father. The saints will be like angels in power and excel in strength.

There will be no death but life will be their food every day. Their food will be life; drinks will be life, clothes will be life, shelters will be life and work will be life. Everything will be life for them.

There is no light off; water shortage, sun heat or any other thing that cause trouble to wellbeing. Life will be fruitful always and joy will be our food every day.

It is an everlasting city and peace reigns all the time. Discouragement; fruitless, burdens, worries and fears will not be heard off. There shall be no motherless; fatherless, widow, orphans in this city.

God shall be our father and mother throughout eternity. We shall see Him face to face and our tears will forever wipe away. We shall rest from all burdens and our good works shall follow us.

Let us fight and enter into the narrow way that leads to life. Let consider this text and discus something about it.

Isaiah 66:6-13

6The sound of noise from the city! A voice from the temple! The voice of the LORD, Who fully repays His enemies!

God will punish those who cause problem for the saints and oppression them. He will fully repay their enemies. Our eyes shall see the suffering of our enemies and they shall be tormented and vanish eternally.

Consider verse 7 and 8 for state that the everlasting city will be in. Read;

7"Before she was in labor, she gave birth; before her pain came, she delivered a male child.

8Who has heard such a thing? Who has seen such things? Shall the earth be made to give birth in one day? Or shall a nation be born at once? For as soon as Zion was in labor, she gave birth to her children.

Means in Zion or New Jerusalem there shall be no pain in anything that we will be doing. Our life shall be free from pain and hardships. Things will be easy and comfort. Whatever we will do, will be in joy and happiness. The situation will be pleasant and peace. Read verse 9 and 10.

9Shall I bring to the time of birth, and not cause delivery?" says the LORD. "Shall I who cause delivery shut up the womb?" says your God.

10"Rejoice with Jerusalem, and be glad with her, all you who love her; Rejoice for joy with her, all you who mourn for her;

Our life will out of pressure and chaos; all things will be easy for us. I mean those who have chance to enter the New Jerusalem. We shall forget the past and it will not come to mind or heart.

Our heart shall fill with joy and we rejoice with angels of heaven. There will be no more hunger but satisfaction. We shall drink deeply with abundance of glory.

We shall be at peace like a river and as the one whom his mother comforts. God will comfort us in the city of Jerusalem. Read verse 11; 12 and 13 and take note of the situation of the saints in the New Jerusalem.

11That you may feed and be satisfied With the consolation of her bosom, That you may drink deeply and be delighted With the abundance of her glory."

12For thus says the LORD: "Behold, I will extend peace to her like a river, And the glory of the Gentiles like a flowing stream. Then you shall feed; on her sides shall you be carried, and be dandled on her knees.

13As one whom his mother comforts, So I will comfort you; And you shall be comforted in Jerusalem."

Let us continue the reading and consider other truth concerning the state of the saints.

Isaiah 65:16-23

Verse 16; we shall bless ourselves in the Lord and shall swear by the Lord of truth. Our trials; our sadness, worries and troubles will be forgotten. It shall be hidden from our eyes and will not remember again. Read;

16So that he who blesses himself in the earth shall bless himself in the God of truth; and he who swears in the earth shall swear by the God of truth; because the former troubles are forgotten, And because they are hidden from my eyes.

This world will be forgotten and shall no more remember. God will create the new one and the former will not come to mind or be remembered. Jerusalem will be a rejoicing city and her people will be a joy.

God shall rejoice with us and there shall be no more weeping or crying. For behold, he has created all things new. The city will be a joyful of city and her people will be a joy.

Death will be no more; everyone will be as God. That is, those who will be in the city. Our labor shall not be in vain. Neither shall anyone be plant for another to eat.

Jerusalem will last for eternity and her people shall also last for eternity. This city has no end; it has the age of God and His glory. Read verse 17 – 23 and consider the end message.

17"For behold, I create new heavens and a new earth; and the former shall not be remembered or come to mind.

18But be glad and rejoice forever in what I create; for behold, I create Jerusalem as a rejoicing, and her people a joy.

19I will rejoice in Jerusalem, and joy in my people; the voice of weeping shall no longer be heard in her, nor the voice of crying.

20"No more shall an infant from there live but a few days, Nor an old man who has not fulfilled his days; For the child shall die one hundred years old, But the sinner being one hundred years old shall be accursed.

21They shall build houses and inhabit them; they shall plant vineyards and eat their fruit. 22They shall not build and another inhabit; they shall not plant and another eat; for as the days of a tree, so shall be the days of my people, And My elect shall long enjoy the work of their hands.

23They shall not labor in vain, nor bring forth children for trouble; for they shall be the descendants of the blessed of the LORD, and their offspring with them.

I know you have heard and read some of the texts by yourself. What is your decision about this matter? How have you considered? What is your goal now? Which city do you wish to dwell?

This world will pass away and it shall never be remembered or comes to mind. New Jerusalem will be replacing by this world. It is a joy and everlasting city.

Money will not be necessary; luxurious cars will not be needed; airplanes will not be considered. Gold will be floor tiles on our foot. What again do you wish than this city?

13. What can we compare?

As God cannot be compare with anything, so is His dwelling place or city. New Jerusalem is the city of God and it is His kingdom. It is a city of His name and glory.

It has no likened and there is nothing that can be associated with from today's world. No human being can explain or describe. It was shown to John as human can know a little about it.

It is because God has prepared something for His love one which has never been in the heart of man or imagine. Who have seen God before and who can describe Him.

As God does not have any equal so is His city prepare for those who love Him. The city has the glory of God and it is also a light to this city. What can you imagine that will be equal to it.

It has been decorated with gold and other precious materials. It has a river of life; it has a tree of life, it has a sea of glass and different kinds of foundations with names of the Apostles written on it.

In it dwells righteousness and justice. It has equal in length; breadth and height. Three gates on each corner with angels; it gates does not shut and the walls are glasses. The sun; moon and stars are absent but only the glory of God is the light in this city.

Temple is not necessary, for God will be with His people and they shall serve Him all the time. Night will be absent; there will be no more pain, there will be no more sickness, there will be no more death.

There will be no more light bills; there will be no more school fees, there will be no more transport fairs, airplanes will not be necessary.

What can you compare or imagine with? No more tax collectors; no more metropolitan's assemblies whose cheat people for their own benefits.

No more militaries, no more police, no more fire service men and no more immigration service. There will no party or politicians who will seek for power. There will be no more prophets; pastors, teachers, magicians, doctors and others.

Supreme Court and high court will be absent and there shall be no more court registrar or secretary. Hospitals will be absent and mortuary will not be present. Harbor and others will be absent. Transports will be no more seen. Communication tools will not be necessary.

Football games and other entertainment will be absent. There will be no more thieves; fornicators, witchcrafts, occult, gangsters and other pleasurable activities.

All these and others that we see in today's world will not be present. This city new Jerusalem holds it peace and comfort. There shall be no more disturbances or any conflict among brothers.

Envy will be lost; murderers will be no more, bribe will not be present and cheating will be forever lost. Today's renowned cities will not be heard off. There shall be no lies; gambling and autocratic acts.

All that we hear and act in today's world will be absent. It is a city of God and anything that is unclean shall not enter. It is a joyful city and peace reigns.

Christ will be our king; leader or president and He will be light; joy and happiness. He shall reign forever and ever. What is your comfort and joy? Are you ready to be in this city?

14. What are you seeking for?

Is there anything that can help you than this? Do you know something important and best than what you have just read? Is the anyplace better or peaceful than what you have heard now?

What is your mind now? What decision are you making to achieve this city? Who is your hope? How can he or she help you? What makes differences between today's world and the new world to come?

What are you seeking for? In fact, you cannot compare anything with the coming world that we have just learnt. It is true and sure with no doubt. The world today and everything in them will pass away.

All that we are doing today will not end in anywhere. Our desire for world good will end in vanity. We will not take to anywhere and it cannot give us life.

All things in the world today are vanity and disturb of mind. Today's fashion will not lead us to anywhere. Beautiful mansions will be as nothing. Cars in today's world will not benefit us. Airplanes will not bring us any joy at end. Who can take these things into grave? Who will last for eternity? Why are we wasting our time on the things that profit nothing? The sweets songs will pass away. Football games will forever end. Money cannot lead us to anywhere and cannot save us.

Big titles or names will be lost. What will benefit you? What do you need most? From east to west; north to south who has been able to reach thousand years of age?

Do you know someone who has live for thousand years before? Who is it? What is his name? Why some of us struggling for world goods which cannot saves life? What shall we benefit from it eternally? Let us consider the saying of the preacher. Ecclesiastes 1:2-4

Read;

2"Vanity of vanities," says the Preacher; "Vanity of vanities, all is vanity." 3What profit has a man from all his labor in which he toils under the sun?

4One generation passes away, and another generation comes; But the earth abides forever.

Whatever we do is vanity and ends in vanity. So, what is the profit for search or struggling for world possessions? Which will save your life or give you life?

In fact, envy has led many people into the place they never thought off and it has ruined their life into beyond repairs. Read verse 6-10 and then continue on the message.

6The wind goes toward the south, and turns around to the north; the wind whirls about continually, and comes again on its circuit.

7All the rivers run into the sea, yet the sea is not full; to the place from which the rivers come, there they return again.

8All things are full of labor; Man cannot express it. The eye is not satisfied with seeing, nor the ear filled with hearing.

9That which has been is what will be, that which is done is what will be done, and there is nothing new under the sun.

10Is there anything of which it may be said, "See, this is new"? It has already been in ancient times before us.

There is nothing which can be benefit us or that can totally satisfy us. Have you asked yourself before why you still seeking for things without rest?

Why I am not satisfied of all the things I have? Why sea cannot become full but it still demanding? Why what you have does not sufficient you? Who have reject abundance of money before? What do we lack most? What do we need to seek for?

In fact, without Christ we shall continue lack and we can do nothing. Your benefit is only Christ and Christ alone.

Why are you searching for food that profits nothing? Will our work take us to somewhere? Or what will be the end results? Read verse 13- 18 and what you will do now.

13And I set my heart to seek and search out by wisdom concerning all that is done under heaven; this burdensome task God has given to the sons of man, by which they may be exercised.

14I have seen all the works that are done under the sun; and indeed, all is vanity and grasping for the wind.

15What is crooked cannot be made straight, and what is lacking cannot be numbered.

16I communed with my heart, saying, "Look, I have attained greatness, and have gained more wisdom than all who were before me in Jerusalem. My heart has understood great wisdom and knowledge."

17And I set my heart to know wisdom and to know madness and folly. I perceived that this also is grasping for the wind.

18For in much wisdom is much grief, and he who increases knowledge increases sorrow.

Our knowledge cannot lead us to anywhere at the end. Our works are grasping for the wind. Means, it will not give us eternal life or fulfill our destiny.

What is crooked cannot be straightened and what is lacking has no limit. Our greatness cannot lead us to anywhere and wisdom cannot save us. Though, we cannot sit there for not doing anything.

But we need to work on it way and seek on it way; planned on it away and eat on it way. In all, it must be glorify God and be on it way. Means, we must be satisfy on the little or the big have we have and thank God for it.

But we should not go beyond the boundary. Whatever we do, whatever we go must be on it way. Means, it must go as the laws of God requires. Everything has it time and everything will end. Today will become yesterday and things that happen will be a history. What will last? Those who do the will of God will last.

What are you seeking for? It is a house? It is a car? It is a husband? It is other belongings? Will it help you than anything you are seeking at the moment? What for? There is time for everything under the sun.

Whatever you are seeking is what you need for the moment. But will it benefit you until when? Men, the world and everything in it will pass away. So, what is the benefit of seeking that thing? You need it; I know you need it, but what way do you need it? What rules governs your desire?

Consider this quote and keep in mind.

To everything there is a season, a time for every purpose under heaven:

A time to be born, and a time to die; a time to plant, and a time to pluck what is planted;

A time to kill, and a time to heal; A time to break down, and a time to build up; A time to weep, and a time to laugh; A time to mourn, and a time to dance;

Ecclesiastes 3:1-4

You need to know that life cannot be, unless you recognize God or Christ. Many people want promotions and positions, others wants to be rich. Some also wants to be fame. People are looking for possessions and other pleasurable things. But what have they considered?

Then I returned and considered all the oppression that is done under the sun: And look! The tears of the oppressed, But they have no comforter—On the side of their oppressors there is power, But they have no comforter.

Therefore I praised the dead who were already dead, more than the living who are still alive.

Yet, better than both is he who has never existed, who has not seen the evil work that is done under the sun. (Ecclesiastes **4:1-3**)

Your only hope is Christ Jesus; He is the one you need to seek for. Do not rely on anything or put trust in any being. They all are vanities and disturbing of mind. Will you seek for Him? Decide now!

15. Will you be among the saints?

Oh dear, there is something great before us. What have you notice? What is your life today? There is a race before us and fight that needs to be winning.

Who can tell the end results of all that we are doing? Who knows what will happen at the moment? There is a word coming and that word needs reply. What will be your position among the thousands?

Will you hear name among the saints? Who shall call you? So, have you think of it that there is a judgment? Many are call, but few will be taking.

Let us see if you will be among the saints? What food do you eat? What dress do you wear? What about your communication? Do you lie? Have you avoided fornication?

Do you still deceive others? Do you pay bribe? Do you receive bribe? Are you a murderer? Do you cheat others on their pay? Are you a thief? What way do you seek for money?

What work do you do? Are you a banker to banker worker? Are you on somebody's husband? Do you respect others? Are you a truly prophet? What minister are you? Have you stopped gambling? How do you respond to others needs? Where from your possessions?

Do you smoke? Have you stop drug abuse? What are you selling? Are you chasing boys or girls? Who is your friend? Are you witchcraft? Are you practicing occultism? Who do you follow?

Do you oppress others because of your money? What do you seek for? What king are you? You can answer these questions for yourself. Your answer will determine your position today if you will be among the saints in the new world.

Many people have taken things for granted and doing what they wish. There many Christians who does not regard the ten commandment of God.

Some also says it is not necessary to keep it. Now, my question to them is what identifies them? Or what is their character? Where do their get religion from?

Who are they following? Every tree has a fruit and the fruit identifies the kind of that tree. Do not be deceived; for God will bring every deed into judgment whether good or bad.

It is true that you are following Christ? Then listen to His words. Why do you call me Lord; Lord, but do not do what I say? If you love me keep my commandments.

Everyone that keeps His words is a wise man who built his house on the rock. The saints will be those who keeps his words whether many or little.

These people will have right to enter into the New Jerusalem. Not all who call me Lord; Lord will enter the kingdom of Heaven, but those who obey His voice.

The outside the city are dogs and sorcerers and sexually immoral and murderers and idolaters, and whoever loves and practices a lie.

But blessed are those who do His commandments that they may have the right to the tree of life, and may enter through the gates into the city.

Now, you can see the sign that makes you a saint among the saints. Will you be part or not? What are you doing now to be part of the righteous?

Here is the patient of the saints and here are those who keep the commandments of God and have faith in Christ.

Never think your works can saves you and do not be a servant who his master set him on his servants and cheat them.

Be faithful and hold the truth that you have now heard from these messages and then do your part as a sin but have done what pleases the master. Consider this text and think of it.

Revelation 22:16-18

Read;

I, Jesus, have sent My angel to testify to you these things in the churches. I am the Root and the Offspring of David, the Bright and Morning Star."

17And the Spirit and the bride say, "Come!" And let him who hears say, "Come!" And let him who thirsts come. Whoever desires, let him take the water of life freely.

18For I testify to everyone who hears the words of the prophecy of this book: If anyone adds to these things, God will add to him the plagues that are written in this book;

For Good Living; salvation and Knowledge Gain!
B. B. S. LIFE BOOKS.

The Gorgeous and Vigorous City | Page

Also by Bernard Benson Sarfo

The Fact Among Facts (1st)
The Fact Among Facts

Standalone
The Youth Murderer
Be Original Not a Copy
The Christians Science or Scholarship
Precious than Paradise
Habit Makes Future
A shelter from storm and rain
The Science of Life
The Strongest Lion Knockback
The Perfect and Inspiring City
Above Hope, Faith and Love
The Hero's Brave Decisions
The Weakest Among Plants
The Hero's Brave Decisions
Doing Above The Ability
The Wisdom Beyond Power And Greatness
Heavier Than the Heavens
The Academics Brains and Recreation Logics
The Strange Voice

The Chaotic World
Don't Miss Your Flight
Let the Nations Ponder
You Are Your Thoughts
I AM has sent me to you
Life Tools
The Fact Among Facts
You Are Glorified
The Life Cinema
The Victims of Lifelong Slavery
The Beauty behind Her Ladyship
The Gorgeous and Vigorous City

About the Author

Bernard Benson Sarfo is an acquainted architectural designer and a motivational speaker.He is a gifted teacher who continues to motivate and encourage many.

Read more at https://www.amazon.com//author/bbslifebooks.